I am

Ainka Moore

I am that I am

Author: Ainka Moore
First Published in 2024
Published by Ainka Moore
ISBN: 978-976-8341-55-6
First Printed in 2024
Cover Design: Books by LR

Email: ainkyjclean@gmail.com
Contact: +18682833123

Dedication

To my mother, to my immediate family and friends.

Table of Content

About The Author

Ainka can be declared as an advocate for love, peace and a meaningful life.

She is indeed divinely gifted. Over the years throughout life's challenges, Ainka developed resilience beyond anything imaginable. A timid girl who once cared about what people thought of her became unbothered and a fiery force to be reckoned with.

A passionate woman with faith that could move mountains and spin the world around, that is Ainka.

Her love for children is unmatched. She has a burning desire to assist with rehabilitation in society and with healing and transformation the lives of many stand at the forefront as her biggest dream.

Her rules are simple but only applicable to the awakened; set boundaries, preserve throughout it all, shut down negativity, love yourself, full your own bucket, be kind, be honest, do everything necessary to protect your mental health and fulfill your purpose!

Why I created this book?

I understand that many persons have a very short attention span and the busyness of life overwhelms us. In this book, the main focus is to captivate the reader with a steady flow of truth and heartfelt emotions.

Simple things should be seen as **BIG** blessings in disguise, I have taken great pride in my delivery towards this craft along with the goal of winning the reader's undivided attention.

This book is highly recommended for persons aged 16 and up, so I encourage anyone who has a burning desire to become the absolute best version of themselves to enjoy reading!

Introduction

God said to Moses, "I am who I am." *Exodus 3:14.*

And he said, "Say this to the people of Israel: 'I am has sent me to you." This powerful declaration from God himself is a living proof to date that the positive affirmative use of letter "I" signifies "Authority".

"I" is the ninth letter of the alphabet and the Roman numeral for one (1). "I" stands-out to me mainly because of its authoritative, insightful, and affirmative dominance whenever it's used in a positive context.

Letter "I" is usually lightly taken, millions of people miss the true essence of life and prematurely abort their "DESTINY." Lack of wisdom, knowledge and understanding can also be factored in as; "Root Causes" for the miscarriages a man may experience. I grew to respect the true power of "I" five years ago while battling some of the roughest storms.

It cost a lot of "gut punching" pains until I finally stood up and said, "I AM NEVER GONNA GIVE UP!"

With God's intervention, selfless support from a few carefully selected and divinely appointed, "destiny helpers" I often called them; I was able soar my way into countless victories.

I stood up
I assessed myself
I surrender to humility
I sought wisdom from the wise
I changed my circle
I stood alone most times
I read
I researched
I sacrificed
I cried
I fell
I got up
I fell again
I cried again
I fell again
I felt excruciating pain
I got up
I crawled sometimes
I was tired
I dragged myself up
I kept going.
I arrived
I won
I cried

I stood out
I will keep going
I have to keep going
I MUST keep going!

Forgiveness

Cleanse the heart and mind from everything wrong that doesn't belong in order to receive.
Forgiveness unblocks held-up blessings and is also your only hope for divine healing.
Forgiving someone who've broken your trust is extremely difficult, but the more you let go, it becomes obvious to recognize that even the meanest of humans suffers within, sometimes even worse than the pain they inflicted upon you.

Forgive Anyway!

I SEE YOU!

I see you King!

I see you Queen!
I see your scars as seeds!
I see your growth beyond gravity!
I see you coming back for everything you once thought was gone forever!
I see the impossible being made possible in your life!
I see you conqueror!
I see the amazing life you're about to create for generations to follow after you!
I see all of your dreams coming through!
I see you completely walking away from your past!
I see you above always and never beneath!
I see all of your fears vanish!
I see you healed and whole again!
I see you as an immaculately beautiful creation!
I see you with wings soaring high like an eagle!
I see flames of untamable fortune in your eyes!
I see the love in your heart that'll never die!

Daily Affirmations

Day 1

I came to conquer I came to survive.

Day 2

No past mistake should have the power to shadow your present achievements.

Day 3

I came to serve my fellow men humbly.

Day 4

Don't give up on anything you're passionate towards.

Day 5

I shall prosper and be in good health.

Day 6

Passion poisons pride and empowers people

Day 7

I shall become and remain teachable

Day 8

Never allow doubting "Thomas" or "Tina" to frustrate you away from your vision.

Day 9

I live a life filled with of favor; I'm a walking miracle.

Day 10

Bury some secrets, kill that desire to overshare your personal life.

Day 11

I am always going to walk in power.

Day 12

Major on the major issues and minor on minor matters.

Day 13

I will treat the poor with compassion and kindness.

Day 14

Take your time with "Today," and create magical moments.

Day 15

I will become a better friend.

Day 16

Speak to your soul and make beautiful and passionate remarks.

Day 17

I will stand against drugs, the abuse of alcohol and substances.

Day 18

Happiness and peace of mind are most priceless.

Day 19

I pride myself in cleanliness.

Day 20

Never cast your pearls to swine, they'll take it back into mud

Day 21

I will prepare a pleasant path for many generations to walk in.

Day 22

Guard you heart around the clock, it can be easily misled and broken.

Day 23

I am harmoniously connected to my inner child.

Day 24

New wine can't be trusted in old wine skin, for better to come rid your life of everything toxic.

Day 25

I will have a beautiful marriage.

Day 26

Choose wisdom over hearsay.

Day 27

I am one of a kind, there's nobody like me.

Day 28

During difficult times cling to faith and push through those storms with confidence.

Day 29

I should be able to take constructive criticism and meaningful action.

Day 30

You shouldn't be left open for just any and everyone, closing some doors are necessary.

Day 31

I am progressing in the moment that I should.

Day 32

Take care of your physical and mental health with the exact same care, attention and gentleness a newborn baby requires.

Day 33

I will not hurt or physically harm anyone.

Day 34

Pride can deceive you, choose humbleness.

Day 35

I will walk away from arguments peacefully.

Day 36

There's no amount of money that's sufficient to purchase real peace.

Day 37

I will make better decisions for my life.

Day 38

Structure, passion and consistency are the key.

Day 39

I love every single piece of "ME".

Day 40

Treat everyone with gentleness, it is warm enough to melt the coldest of hearts.

Day 41

I will love, respect and honor my elders.

Day 42

When you learn teach and while you're teaching learn.

Day 43

I am always going take care of my mental health.

Day 44

Prayer is your only way in and out

Day 45

I am a respecter of all race and religions.

Day 46

Find the "root cause" of situations without casting judgement.

Day 47

I will be a great example for my generation.

Day 48

That almost "Unbearable Pain" you feel today could be your "POWER" tomorrow.

Day 49

I will pronounce beautiful blessings upon everyone I come into contact with

Day 50

Become so self-sufficient that the outside noise is silenced every time your feet hit the ground.

Day 51

I will love and protect all the amazing children of the world.

Day 52

Be kind, kindness makes you glow and grow.

Day 53

I will become the lender not the borrower.

Day 54

Respect the elderly, protect children, rescue animals.

Day 55

I represent unity.

Day 56

"Giving" should become a part of your life's purpose and passion.

Day 57

I am a living legacy.

Day 58

Rid your life of the torment worrying creates

Day 59

I will continuously seek after divine wisdom.

Day 60

Step to the forefront and operate with authority

Day 61

I will prosper beyond all doubt and fear.

Day 62

You must first become the living proof of everything "great" you desire to teach.

Day 63

I will learn about wise investments.

Day 64

Sit at seashores, marvel at mountain tops and smile every time you see a butterfly.

Day 65

I will corporate with my higher self.

Day 66

Simple things are priceless privileges you shouldn't take for granted.

Day 67

I do understand the struggles less fortunate people face.

Day 68

See "Earth" as a vineyard, diligently work in it and positively impact the lives of others.

Day 69

I bask in the beauty of righteousness.

Day 70

Without wisdom one becomes fragile and easily blown as dust into the wind.

Day 71

I will not make wild judgmental assumptions.

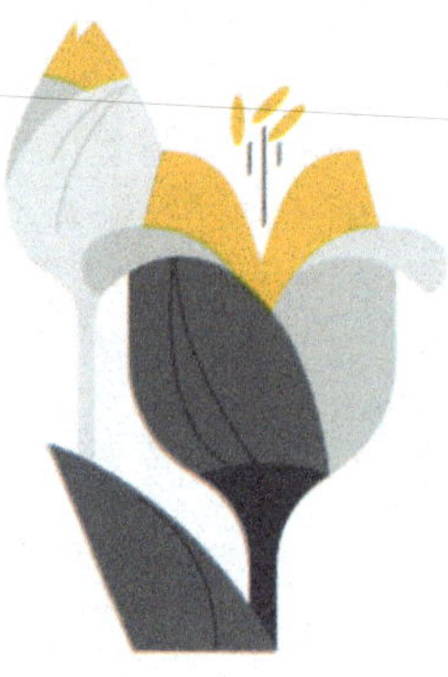

Day 72

A burnt boy should now be fully aware of fire.

Day 73

I help people identify and connect deeply with their true purpose.

Day 74

Convert selfishness into selflessness

Day 75

I understand the importance of proper parenting.

Day 76

Sleep well, eat well, dress well, speak well and operate with authority!

Day 77

I will share positivity wherever I go.

Day 78

Eat all, drink all, have all, see all, know all but never talk all. "Grandpa Chance" saying

Day 79

I will outshine myself daily.

Day 80

Decide you're going to do it and just get it done

Day 81

I do believe in true love.

Day 82

You are more, I am more, they are more, we are more so it is more.

Day 83

I am healed and I am whole.

Day 84

Bury yourself in love and endless peace shall flow through your veins

Day 85

I will always forgive others and ask of their forgiveness.

Day 86

Angles rejoice every time you smile.

Day 87

I am secure within the boundaries I created.

Day 88

Ego can destroy the most beautiful experiences if it's not removed from your character.

Day 89

I will ensure outermost safety of the vulnerable.

Day 90

Master emotional intelligence.

Day 91

I am a protector of harmony.

Day 92

Lock in wholeheartedly with your creativity.

Day 93

I can strategize and materialize.

Day 94

Always keep wanting more for yourself.

Day 95

I despise everything evil and negative.

Day 96

Protect yourself at all level.

Day 97

I am held at high esteem by the right people.

Day 98

Become uncontrollably determined and passionate about yourself.

Day 99

I am not afraid to take a risk.

Day 100

Understand that the past will forever be the past. Accept it.

Day 101

I am not afraid to start over.

Day 102

Go back and go deep; release every emotion you have tried covering up or had difficulty facing.

Day 103

I have to work more and talk less.

Day 104

Meditate…stay alone a bit, find the time for self-reflection and love.

Day 105

I am in position and this position is my power.

Day 106

Don't stay too long where you don't belong.

Day 107

I attract people who're healthy for my soul.

Day 108

You can relocate, if possible, change of scenery since the environment plays an essential part of rebuilding one's life.

Day 109

I love the air that I breathe.

Day 110

There is divine magic hidden inside of you; tap in! The world awaits.

Day 111

I will enjoy everything good on earth.

Day 112

Partner with likeminded people willing to help you climb the mountain of faith.

Day 113

I count on love to survive.

Day 114

Never be afraid to ask for help.

Day 115

I understand that every day is a gift.

Day 116

Dream beyond boundaries and live unapologetically all for the sake of a fruitful, fulfilling life.

Day 117

I will set myself up for the "Win".

Day 118

Be sure never to take the simple things is life for granted.

Day 119

I shut down every thought of doubt.

Day 120

We are all privileged beings destined for and deserving of fulfilling journey.

Day 121

I am not ashamed of my past mistakes.

Day 122

Life is not easy, the experiences each of us become more willing to share would aid in lessening its burdens.

Day 123

I am blossoming beautifully.

Day 124

Create a safer space for continuous growth.

Day 125

I will encourage others to heal and speak positively about themselves.

Day 126

The only regret from a mistake you should have been not learning from it.

Day 127

I cannot finish what never started.

Day 128

So, my friends let us pick beautiful flowers of every kind.

Day 129

I am maturing in all areas of life.

Day 130

Bathe in the rain occasionally, receive your showers of blessings.

Day 131

I would turn pain into power.

Day 132

Dance along to sweet sounding melodies from birds of the fields.

Day 133

I will not allow my past to negatively affect my future.

Day 134

Gaze at sunsets and never forget how free we all are.

Day 135

I connect deeply and passionately with nature.

Day 136

Chase after butterflies as you discover your joys of life.

Day 137

I will experience supernatural increase.

Day 138

Explore the world to open your eyes.

Day 139

I will exceedingly pass every exam given.

Day 140

God has given me everything that I would ever want and need.

Day 141

I embrace my true potential.

Day 142

My network and net worth work together.

Day 143

I am soaring higher than I would have ever imagined.

Day 144

Capitalize on sensible opportunities.

Day 145

I understand the importance of honesty.

Day 146

Embrace the fountain of great fortune.

Day 147

I understand the consequences of dishonesty.

Day 148

Focus on building for the generations that come after me.

Day 149

I will strive towards becoming more loyal.

Day 150

Keep shining brighter than yesterday.

Day 151

I am wonderfully created, and I am enough.

Day 152

Don't ever stop growing.

Day 153

I possess an overwhelming desire for the development of all.

Day 154

Give to those not expecting a return favor.

Day 155

I will go above and beyond for the further development of my life.

Day 156

Forever shut down negativity.

Day 157

I won't listen to anything else other than positivity.

Day 158

Believe in positivity.

Day 159

I am determined to clean up whatever mess I make.

Day 160

Bulldoze all barriers and blockages.

Day 161

I will win in this season.

Day 162

Create a beautiful home with beautiful music and laughter.

Day 163

I will sit on the throne of marriage; my king will find me.

Day 164

Show compassion towards all.

Day 165

I am a living “Legend” and “Legacy” of the ancients.

Day 166

Look for lessons hidden in all things.

Day 167

I have everything it takes to make a difference in the world.

Day 168

Life is ever learning; always learn something new.

Day 169

I will protect my mental health.

Day 170

Be not ashamed to cry.

Day 171

I will not get lost into the system.

Day 172

Bring solutions to problems or say nothing at all.

Day 173

I am the woman or man that generations to come would never be able to stop talking about.

Day 174

Create solid foundations for the various pillars that will support my function.

Day 175

I am addicted to bettering myself.

Day 176

Embrace my natural beauty with pure love and appreciation.

Day 177

I am the firefighter not the fire.

Day 178

Make plans but hold them lightly because God has the final say.

Day 179

I am connected to my true essence.

Day 180

Appreciate simplicity.

Day 181

I understand the significance of my contribution to life's purpose.

Day 182

Learn about the importance of creating generational wealth.

Day 183

I will never lack productivity.

Day 184

Get into environments that value me.

Day 185

I am the chef not the ingredients.

Day 186

Put a demand on greatness.

Day 187

I am strong enough to be gentle.

Day 188

Be gentle, understanding that everyone is wired differently.

Day 189

I am in alignment with God.

Day 190

Practice doing what is good.

Day 191

I will think long and deep before I speak.

Day 192

Remain teachable.

Day 193

I will continuously raise the bar.

Day 194

Prosper and be in good health.

Day 195

I will run through troops and leap over walls.

Day 196

Overcome fears with faith.

Day 197

I am qualified beyond the naked eyes.

Day 198

Continue to evolve.

Day 199

I will increase my listening ability.

Day 200

Receive goodness and mercy all the days of my life.

Day 201

I own my mind so I will take good care of it.

Day 202

Effortlessly attract permanent abundance.

Day 203

I will never stop praying and praising Almighty God.

Day 204

Sow seeds of love into the lives of others.

Day 205

I am divinely inspired.

Day 206

Start and end each year victorious.

Day 207

I will matter to people who connect to my purpose.

Day 208

See light instead of darkness.

Day 209

I will no longer procrastinate I will finish what I started.

Day 210

Take responsibility my decisions and the consequences.

Day 211

I shine brightly amongst amazing stars.

Day 212

Seek wisdom daily.

Day 213

I own my uniqueness.

Day 214

Be a great example to many.

Day 215

I will communicate respectfully.

Day 216

Love everyone unconditionally.

Day 217

I only want the best out of life.

Day 218

Laugh and enjoy the goodness of life.

Day 219

I am capable of evolving.

Day 220

Always be victorious.

Day 221

I am wonderfully and uniquely created.

Day 222

Remember the poor and treat them with love and kindness.

Day 223

I can do all the great things my heart desires.

Day 224

Sow positive deeds to reap bountifully.

Day 225

I am be seated in high places.

Day 226

Always remain humble.

Day 227

I believe in myself.

Day 228

Each day learn from all of my mistakes.

Day 229

I am a survivor no matter the outcome.

Day 230

Always attract beautiful things into my life.

Day 231

I will live an abundant life filled with peace.

Day 232

Believe in my potential.

Day 233

I get excited when others succeed.

Day 234

Have everything it takes to win.

Day 235

I embrace challenges and changes; I will work harder.

Day 236

Positive vibes only in my life.

Day 237

I understand how powerful and effective words are.

Day 238

Give honor where honor is due.

Day 239

I will make a remarkable difference in this world.

Day 240

Pronounce beautiful blessings upon everyone I connect with.

Day 241

I will continue to stand out.

Day 242

Possess contagious joy.

Day 243

I am loved, so love will always find me.

Day 244

Be an extraordinary human being.

Day 245

I represent peace and unity.

Day 246

Cherish each day as your last.

Day 247

I belong to a beautiful tribe of souls.

Day 248

Each day thrive on love.

Day 249

I am progressing, so I will be supportive of others.

Day 250

Shine brilliant like a star.

Day 251

I am a believer of love.

Day 252

Keep faith alive.

Day 253

I cannot be hindered or stopped.

Day 254

Do the right things even when no one is looking.

Day 255

I lack no good thing.

Day 256

Positively contribute to society.

Day 257

I take pride in cleanliness.

Day 258

Harness the ability to control my emotions.

Day 259

I am a blessing to many generations.

Day 260

Operate with the "Authority" which God has given.

Day 261

I have a soul filled with love and sunshine.

Day 262

Be open to new ideas.

Day 263

I am loved and cherished by the right people.

Day 264

Stay always above and never beneath.

Day 265

I am advancing in life.

Day 266

Walk away from negativity and conflicts.

Day 267

Continuous growth is important.

Day 268

Each day protect my peace.

Day 269

I know that God is in control.

Day 270

Embrace continuous growth.

Day 271

I am progressing seamlessly by the grace of God.

Day 272

Do not pretend to be anybody that I am not.

Day 273

I am taking full charge of my body by treating it well.

Day 274

Demonstrating building blocks to a positive mindset.

Day 275

I am a divine force.

Day 276

Be calm and comfortable.

Day 277

I am winning every race in the game of life.

Day 278

Accept constructive criticism.

Day 279

I will exhale fear and inhale courage.

Day 280

The Lord is my Sheperd. I shall not want.

Day 281

I am too blessed to be stressed.

Day 282

Show me wisdom and strength to overcome my trials.

Day 283

I harmoniously connect with my inner child.

Day 284

Kindness always wins.

Day 284

I am thankful for the gift of life.

Day 286

Being kind is not a sign of weakness.

Day 287

I am everything great plus humble.

Day 288

Kindness is a strength that is greatly underrated

Day 289

I am self-sufficient and rooted in love.

Day 290

Kindness mixed with a little iron fist is a nice blend

Day 291

I respect every creed and race.

Day 292

Accept flaws and imperfections because that what's make me be me.

Day 293

I respect myself and all around me.

Day 294

Find the courage to leave the table if respect is no longer being served.

Day 295

I am a champion.

Day 296

Take life one step at a time.

Day 297

I am making a positive impact in many people's live.

Day 298

Be positive and powerful

Day 299

I am invincible.

Day 300

Remember the value you bring to the table.

Day 301

I won't be long where I don't belong.

Day 302

Surround yourself with people who value and respect you.

Day 303

I will overcome that addiction.

Day 304

Know your worth.

Day 305

I have a beautiful family.

Day 306

Courage does not always roar.

Day 307

I am qualified for the job

Day 308

Try again tomorrow.
Never give up!

Day 309

I will give thanks and praises all the days of my life.

Day 310

Leadership is not all about being in charge.

Day 311

I do not have to worry. God is in control.

Day 312

Stop wishing. Start doing.

Day 313

I am powerful since my strength comes from God.

Day 314

Remember to have fun and enjoy the journey.

Day 315

I am healing daily.

Day 316

Remember you will have good seasons and bad ones, just prepare for the weather.

Day 317

I am a born leader.

Day 318

Lead by example.

Day 319

I will make it!

Day 320

Never stop being a leader.

Day 321

I am a conqueror!

Day 322

Make kindness a habit.

Day 323

I represent peace.

Day 324

Remove the weeds in your life.

.

Day 325

I represent faith.

Day 326

Live life, live good.

Day 327

I represent prosperity.

Day 328

Nothing can dim the light that shines within.

Day 329

I am a child of the King!

Day 340

What I have done today was the best I was able to do today.

Day 341

I am highly esteemed and well-favored.

Day 342

This my time to shine.

Day 343

I am elevating.

Day 344

Start and maintain good habits

Day 345

I appreciate the beauty of the sunrise and sunset.

Day 346

Remain calm even when feeling annoyed.

Day 347

I possess all my possessions that was bestowed upon me.

Day 348

My hard work will pay off.

Day 348

I will beat all forms of illness.

Day 350

Learn to love life.

Day 351

I will overcome all sickness and disease.

Day 352

Do it today, not tomorrow.

Day 353

I am at the right place at the right time, doing the right thing.

Day 354

Get it done!

Day 355

I am good enough!

Day 356

Each moment of this new day brings opportunities for happiness.

Day 357

I am an unstoppable force of nature.

Day 358

With all the necessary skills and experience, I am the perfect candidate for this job.

Day 359

I wake up motivated every day you.

Day 360

My life has meaning and so do

Day 361

I am aligned with my highest purpose.

Day 362

Today I choose to be happy.

Day 363

I attract positivity and repel negativity.

Day 364

Health, wealth, and harmony are entering my life.

Day 365

My heart is in the right place.

A space for your thoughts

Made in the USA
Columbia, SC
06 June 2025